Destiny's
OPTIC ILLUSION

Look for these and other books about Linelle Destiny in the Linelle Destiny Series:

Visit www.thesecretsistersclub.com

Linelle Destiny Series

Destiny's
OPTIC ILLUSION

Dr. Alicia Holland
Illustrations by Anoop PC

This book may be ordered through booksellers or by contacting:

iGlobal Educational Services, LLC
PO Box 94224
Phoenix, AZ 85070
www.iglobaleducation.com
512-761-5898

Linelle Destiny Series: **Destiny's Optic Illusion**

ISBN-13: 978-1-944346-18-8

Acknowledgements

I want to first honor God for placing in my heart to share my story with others. It was He whom brought Karen and I together to manifest this project. I am so grateful for Karen Hendry as she took my notes and helped write this fictitious book. There are truly no words to express my gratitude as you are truly a blessing.

I also want to thank Surendra Gupta for his creativity in formatting and Anoop PC for his creativity in bringing life to the designs and illustrations in this book series. Both of you are amazing!

Dedication

I dedicate this book series to my beautiful and talented daughters, Georgia and Amaiya Johnson. Remember, you are valued, loved, and competent. You are worthy!

Part 1:
New School Year

Chapter 1
Rough Start

✧ ✧ ✧

Arms full, Destiny pushes the school door open and heads inside. A new school year is about to begin and Destiny is going to spend the day preparing. She has spent some time away from her new baby, Georgia Linelle. There were days during the summer when she was in Florida for her PhD residency that she didn't see her for four or five hours at a time. Still, she feels nervous about being away all day.

"That's part of being a momma," Momma had said when they spoke on the phone last night. "You gonna miss that baby like crazy, but she'll be fine and so will you."

Destiny puts down her box of supplies and books in the hallway outside the office and goes in to check her mailbox. Principal Brandfather is there with Sheree, the school secretary. "Hi Sheree. Hi Daniella. How was your summer," asks Destiny.

"Oh, honey, mine was just fine," says Sheree. "What about yours? How's that new baby doing?"

"She is just great," answers Destiny.

"You are going to bring her in to see us, right?" says Sheree. Destiny can tell by the tone in her voice that she won't accept no for an answer.

"Of course, I will. Later this week."

"Destiny, can I speak with you for a moment?" asks Principal Brandfather, completely ignoring Destiny's question about her summer and talk about the baby.

"Yeah, sure," says Destiny. As Destiny follows Principal Brandfather into her office, she looks over at Sheree, who just shrugs.

"What did you want to speak to me about?" asks Destiny, once Principal Brandfather has shut the door behind them.

"Well, to be honest, I'm concerned about what your performance will be like this year."

"I don't understand."

"You have a new baby and being a mother is a very demanding job. I'm concerned that you won't be able to keep up or produce the results you produced last year."

"Oh, no, Daniella. Don't worry about that," says Destiny. "I'll be just fine. You won't see any difference at all. After all, new mothers work all the time. I'll make it work."

"Well, I certainly hope so. I'd hate to see your students suffer because you aren't up to the task."

Destiny's brow furrows. She has no idea where this is coming from. Surely other teachers at this school have had babies.

"I most certainly am up to the task," says Destiny with a slight edge to her voice.

"Very well, then. I'll let you get to your prep."

Destiny leaves the office, Sheree looking at her with an apologetic face, as if she wishes she could have given Destiny a heads-up about that little confrontation. But Destiny knows it isn't Sheree's fault. Destiny gathers her box and heads to her classroom.

✧ ✧ ✧

Destiny drops the box on her desk and puts her purse away. As she begins to unpack the contents of the box, she thinks about what Principal Brandfather said. *Why is she so concerned that having a new baby will affect my performance*, thinks Destiny.

Then Destiny remembers what she had heard her colleagues saying when she stood outside the staffroom door during the last week of school in May. Richard had said Principal Brandfather doesn't like Destiny and he wouldn't be surprised if she found a way to get rid of her. *Is she planning to use the baby as an excuse? Is she planning to watch me like a hawk and find a reason to fire or demote me?*

Destiny feels sick. She just doesn't understand what Principal Brandfather has against her. Destiny has really helped her students. The proof is plain for anyone to see. In fact, Destiny has helped the school's overall reputation.

Then, Destiny realizes it doesn't matter whether Principal Brandfather likes her or not. She is good at her job and no one can change that or dispute it. And that isn't going to change simply because she is now a mother.

Destiny sits down and begins to prepare for her new school year. She'll show Principal Brandfather just exactly what she's made of. She will get *better* results this year than she did last year. Nothing can stand in her way.

✧ ✧ ✧

Destiny goes home for dinner. She is able to spend an hour with Georgia and Calix before heading off to the tutoring center. But she decides to take Georgia with her. After spending all day away from her, she wants to be near her, even if she has to work with her students.

Besides, everyone who works at the center has met Georgia and they all love her. The staff takes turns holding her and rocking her to sleep. It's like Georgia has half a dozen babysitters just waiting to take care of her.

School hasn't started yet, but there is a steady flow of students through the center that evening. Destiny spends a lot of time greeting students she hasn't seen in a few weeks and the students and their parents all want to see Georgia. Everyone loves babies!

But soon, Destiny has to leave Georgia with staff and make her rounds, helping students, observing her staff, and speaking with parents about their children's progress. A number of new families come in throughout the evening and Destiny greets each one of them, answering their questions, explaining her methods and results, and signing every family up for tutoring.

As the evening is drawing to a close, Destiny realizes she has been so busy, she hasn't seen to Georgia for quite a while. She goes to her office to check on her and finds her sleeping in her car seat, Annalise gently rocking her and pressing a finger against her lips with a smile.

Georgia really likes Annalise. Destiny suspects its Annalise's friendly, free nature and her brilliantly colored clothing that does the trick. Plus, Annalise always wears wonderful beaded bracelets that she lets Georgia play with.

Destiny nods and heads back out to the main room. She stands for a moment and looks around. It has been so busy and it will only get busier once the school year begins. Destiny always finds her enrollment explodes during the first three or four weeks of school and the center is already so busy she is having a difficult time being where she needs to be.

Destiny realizes she needs to determine what is the best use of her time is when it comes to the center. She has staff that can handle the general tutoring of the students and even staff to work with special needs students. She needs to focus on new families and students and perhaps work with some of the students that are struggling more. Plus, she has to work on developing new methods and curriculum.

Shelley comes over and stands beside Destiny. "Busy, isn't it?" she says.

Destiny nods. "I was actually just wondering how to handle it. It's only going to get busier, so I need to decide where to put my focus."

"I'll tell you what you need," says Shelley. "You need an office assistant, someone who can take calls, schedule appointments, answer general questions, and take families through the signup process once they have made the decision. That way you don't have to be right on the front line and can focus on the things you need to focus on."

"You know what? You're right. That's exactly what I need. If I have someone on the front desk, that will free up so much of my time. I don't know why I didn't think of it before."

"Honestly, you could have used an office assistant as soon as you moved into this space, even before you hired Annalise and I."

"You're probably right about that. I already feel like a weight has been lifted off my shoulders just having made the decision to hire someone."

"Good because I need to speak with you about a couple of students."

"Okay. Let's go over to that corner," Destiny points to an empty table on the far side of the room. "Georgia is sleeping in my office and I don't want to disturb her."

Once she is finished talking to Shelley, Destiny goes into her office and gets on her computer. She places an advertisement for an office assistant in the local newspaper. Then she breathes a sigh of relief.

She looks down at Georgia, sleeping peacefully, and just enjoys looking at her gentle face and tiny hands. What a miracle she is. "Well, little one. We will have to figure out how to make this work. But we will. Don't you worry about that. You'll just be spending a lot of time at this center with me as you grow up."

Destiny smiles. Then Dustin, one of her tutors, pops his head into her office. Brushing the long bangs out of his face, he says, "There's a new family out here asking questions."

Destiny stands up and glances down at Georgia one last time. Then she says, "Lead the way." She feels ready to take on the world, no matter what challenges lie ahead. Not a busy tutoring center or even Principal Brandfather can hold her back.

Chapter 2
Hiring

✧ ✧ ✧

Friday has arrived and Destiny feels prepared for the beginning of the school year that will arrive on Monday. She has one more glorious weekend before she greets her new students for the year. Before she heads up to her classroom that morning, Destiny pops into the office.

Sheree is working at her desk and looks up as Destiny walks in. "Hello, there," Sheree says. "I just can't get that adorable baby of yours out of my mind." Destiny had brought Georgia in to the office yesterday so everyone could see her. "She is getting so big."

"I know it," Destiny replies. "It's amazing how fast they grow. Is Daniella in?"

"Yes, she's on the phone at the moment, though."

"I'll wait. I have a question for her."

"Sure thing, darling. But be warned, she seems to be in a mood today."

"She is everyday these days, at least with me, it seems."

Sheree smiles sympathetically and goes back to her work, while Destiny checks her mailbox. A couple of minutes later, Sheree says, "She's off the phone now."

"Thanks," says Destiny, walking over and knocking on Principal Brandfather's door.

"Come in." Principal Brandfather's voice sounds faint behind the closed door.

Destiny opens the door and walks in. Principal Brandfather looks up from the paperwork in front of her and there is a quick grimace that crosses her face at the sight of Destiny.

"What can I do for you, Destiny?"

"Good morning," says Destiny, ignoring Principal Brandfather's rude avoidance of a proper greeting. "Last night while I was working with a student at my tutoring center, I had a thought about the new curriculum we are developing. I..."

"You run a tutoring center?" asks Principal Brandfather. Her voice is cold and precise.

"Yes," Destiny replies. "I have run one since before I moved to Texas. Actually, I've been tutoring since I was in high school."

"Why?"

Destiny realizes Principal Brandfather is dead serious when she asks this question and she is confused. What is the big deal with her tutoring? "Because I love helping kids learn," she replies. "I always have."

"I am honestly surprised," says Principal Brandfather. "Why on earth do you think you have any business tutoring students? You can barely keep up with your duties here, let alone being a new mother."

At first, Destiny doesn't know what to say. Why is Principal Brandfather attacking her like this? Then she gathers her thoughts and says, "I am very good at managing a full work-load. I have been doing this for a long time. I ran the center while I earned my degrees without any trouble. My center has even been awarded a government contract, which brings me back to the question I had about curriculum."

"A government contract? In Texas? But your degrees are from Louisiana? They have no merit here. I don't even know why our school board hired you."

"Hang on," says Destiny. "Just because I got my degrees in Louisiana doesn't mean they are any less than if I had received them here in Texas. I went to legitimate universities and worked very hard for what I earned."

"Yes, yes, I'm sure you did, but in my opinion, you still don't deserve to be teaching here."

"Well, I am."

"Yes, it seems you are. That matter is out of my hands, at least for the time being."

Destiny feels paralyzed, her hands balled into fists at her sides. She takes a deep breath, turns, and walks right out of Principal Brandfather's office, forgetting her question and trying very hard to stay calm.

"Is everything okay?" asks Sheree as Destiny darts through the main office. She doesn't answer and leaves Sheree sitting there staring after her. It's all she can do not to burst into tears. There is no way she can talk to anyone right now.

✧ ✧ ✧

Destiny spent a good chunk of that Friday morning nursing a cup of tea at the diner. She needed to calm down before she could go back into the school. When she did, she made every effort to avoid Principal Brandfather.

Destiny had told Calix about what Principal Brandfather had said to her and he was every bit as angry as she was. He wanted to go into the school and give her a piece of his mind, but Destiny stopped him and got him to calm down.

Now, Destiny is sitting in her office at the tutoring center. It's quiet because the center isn't due to open for an hour. She came in early to get some things done before the students started coming in, but she can't stop thinking about Principal Brandfather's words.

Principal Brandfather is in a position of leadership. She is supposed to support her teachers, not tear them down. *How can she possibly say or even think such things about me?* wonders Destiny.

Then Destiny realizes that it really doesn't matter what Principal Brandfather or anyone else thinks. She knows the merit of her education and her talent and ability as a teacher. What does Principal Brandfather really know about her? Nothing.

Besides, people who lash out at others the way Principal Brandfather has are often dealing with their own personal issues. Destiny considers this and begins to feel bad for Principal Brandfather. What on earth has happened in her life that she is this bitter with Destiny? Destiny shrugs. There is clearly nothing she can do to help Principal Brandfather, at least not at this point. So, she decides she had better help herself stay afloat with a principal who doesn't like her.

Destiny realizes she hasn't yet checked the messages on the center's voice mail. She listens and there is a message from a high school girl named Reginae Jackson. She is interested in the office assistant job.

Destiny smiles. Yes, she is doing just fine, no matter what Principal Brandfather says. She is helping kids and she is employing people. She is doing everything right.

✧ ✧ ✧

Three days later, Destiny is working with a student at the center, waiting for the high school student who applied for the office assistant position. They had set up an interview for this evening and Destiny is looking forward to it. Reginae seemed lovely when they spoke on the phone.

The door to the center opens and Destiny looks up to see a short brown-haired girl walk in. *That must be her,* thinks Destiny, *and she's ten minutes early. It's a good start.*

Destiny asks one of her tutors to take over for her and goes over to greet Reginae. She holds out her hand and says, "Hi, Reginae. It's nice to meet you."

"It's nice to meet you,too, Ms. Sycamores," says Reginae, returning Destiny's handshake.

"Please, call me Destiny," Destiny says as she gestures for Reginae to follow her to her office. "We aren't that formal around here."

"Okay."

Once in Destiny's office and seated at a table in the corner, Destiny observes Reginae. She seems nervous, but well-dressed in a pair of jeans and a light-yellow blouse. Her hair is pulled back in a pony tail.

"So, Reginae, tell me about yourself."

"Sure," she says. "Well, I'm in grade 10, but you already know that." She shifts in her chair a bit. "And I'm really good in math. I have a 98% average right now and I had the top math mark in my class last year."

"That's great," says Destiny, impressed. "What about your interests. What do you enjoy and what do you want to do in the future."

"Well, I love tutoring. I help students at my school all the time."

"I did that when I was in high school, too," says Destiny.

"Cool. I also love hairdressing, which I know isn't really related to math, but it's fun. I'm not really sure what I want to do with my future, though. There are so many options."

"I see," says Destiny. This is a very bright girl sitting across from her. Destiny can see that and she wants to help Reginae see the options that are in front of her. Of course, there isn't anything wrong with wanting to be a hairdresser, but there is so much a girl with her intelligence and talent can do, Destiny wants to be sure to help her see that.

"As we discussed on the phone, the position I am filling is for an office assistant," says Destiny. "That means you will primarily be answering the phone, scheduling appointments, and answering questions from clients and potential clients."

"That's fine," says Reginae.

"Having said that, you will make a good backup tutor whenever we might need one."

"I would love to help with the tutoring!"

Destiny smiles and says, "Reginae, I think you will fit in very well here at the center."

"Really? I have the job?"

"You most certainly do," says Destiny. "What hours can you work?"

"I can work every day after school except Wednesdays because that's when I tutor at school. And I can work on the weekends."

"Super. Can you start tomorrow?"

"I sure can!"

"Great. Why don't you come out with me and meet some of the staff? Then when you come in tomorrow, I'll have a schedule ready for you so you will know your hours."

"How many hours a week will I work?"

"I think we will start with five or six and go from there. I will need you on Saturdays, which is when I greet a lot of new students and families. And Tuesdays for an hour or two."

"Thank you so much," says Reginae.

Destiny smiles as they leave her office. The staff seems to like Reginae when they meet her and Destiny knows she will make a good addition to her team.

Chapter 3
Under a Watchful Eye

✧ ✧ ✧

Destiny is standing outside her classroom one Wednesday afternoon. The last class of the day is over and Destiny is saying goodbye to her students.

"Excuse me, Mrs. Sycamores?" says a voice from behind Destiny. Destiny turns around to see Raelynn standing behind her. Raelynn was one of Destiny's students last year.

"Hi, Raelynn," says Destiny. "How are you doing this year?"

"I'm doing great! Math is going so well, thanks to you."

"I'm glad to hear that. So, what can I do for you?"

"Well," says Raelynn, "I was wondering if you were going to hold another Secret Sister's Community Event. I loved the last one so much and I would like to help organize it. If you need to help, of course."

"That's so nice of you, Raelynn. Unfortunately, I am just too busy to be able to organize it, even with help from great students like you." As she speaks to Raelynn, Destiny can see Principal Brandfather standing at the end of the hall. She is chatting with the occasional student, but Destiny can see that she keeps looking down the hall at her. *She is actually standing there watching me*, thinks Destiny.

She tries to focus on what Raelynn is saying, "Oh, you must be busy then. You know, to not hold another event."

"Yes, well, I have the new baby and teaching. I am also doing my PhD and I have my tutoring center."

"Wow! No wonder you don't have time for the Secret Sister's event. I understand, but when you do hold one again, please let me know. I really want to help."

"Thanks," says Destiny with a smile. "I will definitely remember that."

Raelynn says goodbye and Destiny can see Principal Brandfather still watching her from the other end of the hallway. Destiny can feel anger beginning to bubble inside her. What on earth does she think she is going to catch Destiny doing?

This is really going too far, thinks Destiny.

✧ ✧ ✧

After Destiny gets ready to go home for the day, she decides to stop into Principal Brandfather's office on the way out. She feels the need to talk to Principal Brandfather and straighten this whole thing out once and for all.

When she goes into the office, Sheree can see she is there to see Principal Brandfather. "She's in there," says Sheree in a low voice, "but I don't know if *you* want to be. That woman has got it in for you, sister. And I have no idea why. You just be careful now, you hear?"

"I will, Sheree. Thanks."

She knocks on Principal Brandfather's door.

"Come in," says Principal Brandfather. Then she looks up and sees Destiny and the look on her face sours.

"Yes," is all she says before looking back down at the paperwork on her desk.

"Daniella," begins Destiny, "I need to know what is going on. You were clearly watching me upstairs today. Why?"

"I told you before that I would be keeping an eye on you and I meant it."

"What are you even looking for? Are you going to show up in my classroom next? I mean, this is ridiculous!"

"Is it? Well, I don't see it that way. I am going to make sure you don't slip up, or that when you do, I catch you."

"You really want me out of here that badly?" asks Destiny, amazed at the hatred coming form Principal Brandfather.

"I do."

Destiny takes a deep breath. There is no way she is going to let Principal Brandfather get away with this. "Well, I can promise you that you will never catch me slipping up because it won't happen. I'm good at my job. I'm good with my students. And I am good with curriculum development."

"We'll see," is all Principal Brandfather says.

Destiny is fuming as she leaves the school. She will not let Principal Brandfather get the best of her.

✧ ✧ ✧

As she begins the drive home, Destiny finds she cannot calm down. She is just too angry. She pulls over into a drug store parking lot and calls the tutoring center to let them know she won't be in right away. Then she pulls back out onto the road and heads toward Katie's house. She needs someone to talk to about this.

When she arrives at Katie's house, she hopes Katie is home and isn't too busy to chat. She rings the doorbell and a moment later, the door opens. Katie is standing there in ripped jeans and a white t-shirt.

"Destiny!" shouts Katie, drawing her into a hug. Then she looks around Destiny. She even looks behind her. "No Georgia?"

"No, just me I'm afraid."

"Well, you'll have to do. Come on in."

They go inside and through to the back. "Don't worry about your shoes," says Katie on the way. They sit on the patio in the back. "Ice tea?" offers Katie.

"Sure, thanks."

When Katie brings out two glasses of ice tea and sits down, Destiny speaks. "So, here's the deal. My principal has it in for me, big time. She hates me and she is literally following me around the school, watching every move I make. It's creepy and infuriating."

"Okay, that's heavy," says Katie. "Why?"

"I think she is jealous of me, quite honestly."

"Well, there is plenty to be jealous of," says Katie with a wink.

"Come on, Katie. I'm serious. She is just looking for a reason to fire me."

"Well, don't give her one."

"That's my plan. I just hope it's a good one. I thought you might be a good second opinion."

"Glad to help. And now on to me. Guess what?"

"What?"

"I met someone!"

"Get out! Who?"

Katie is beaming. Her whole face is smiling. "His name is Fred and he's a basketball player."

"So, tall then?"

"Well, yeah. And so cute! He has the most amazing eyes, just like a puppy dog's. I know that sounds cliché, but it's true."

"That is so great," says Destiny. "I'm really happy for you."

"I want you to meet him."

"Yeah, sure, I'd love to."

"Can you come to one of his games?" I think he has one this weekend.

"I can't this weekend," says Destiny, "but soon. I promise."

"I'm holding you to that. You absolutely have to meet him."

"I will, I will. But right now, I should probably go. They can do without me at the center tonight so I think I'll just head home and spend some time with my family."

"Good idea. Get some baby love and see that man of yours."

Destiny hugs Katie at the front door. "Thanks for the ear and the advice."

"Anytime. And I'll be calling about going to a game soon."

"Definitely."

Destiny drives home and unwinds with her family. It feels nice to take a small break.

Part 2
Workload Stress

Chapter 4

The Game Player

✧ ✧ ✧

A couple of weeks pass by and Destiny is feeling the pressure of all her commitments. Principal Brandfather is still watching her closely, frequently making excuses to be on her floor and even visiting the classroom a couple of times. Destiny has been very careful to be on top of her game, but the pressure from work, the tutoring center, and her PhD are mounting.

On top of it all, Georgia is teething and has been cranky and up frequently the past three nights. But at least Destiny and Calix have found a babysitter in the neighborhood, a 19-year-old girl named Jennifer who lives down the street and is very responsible. That means they can go out and Destiny decides a night out would be a good idea.

Katie has been begging Destiny to come out to one of Fred's basketball games so she and Calix book the sitter and make plans for a Friday night out. Destiny is so excited as they arrive at the game. She and Calix meet Katie at the door. Julie is with her.

"Destiny! Calix! I'm so glad you could make it! I have tickets for everyone here."

"Hi," says Calix.

"Hey," says Destiny, giving Katie a hug. "Hi, Julie."

"Hi, Destiny," says Julie. They don't hug, but at least Julie is being civil, even friendly these days. After their falling out a couple of years ago, Destiny wasn't sure they would ever speak again.

They go into the game and take their courtside seats. "Great seats," says Calix.

"Yeah," says Katie. "It helps when you're dating the star player of the home team."

"Which one is he?" asks Destiny, looking at all the tall, handsome basketball players gathered around and listening intently to their coach.

"See the one standing to the right of the coach? That's him." At that moment, Fred looks up briefly and smiles. Katie waves. She is so happy and Destiny is happy for her. It is about time Katie had some love in her life.

The game begins and the action is nonstop. Fred scores his first basket and Katie jumps out of her seat she is cheering so hard. At one point, Fred fouls another player and they almost get into a fight. The player on the other team, number 12, gets to take a free throw, but he misses. Fred scores three more baskets during the game and his team wins.

Katie is cheering wildly and Destiny is, too. She feels so relaxed, which is such a change from how she has felt lately. It is just so nice to get away.

✧ ✧ ✧

Once the game has officially ended, Katie says, "I'll be right back.

She rushes over to see Fred and Calix says, "That was a great game. Fred's pretty good."

"Yeah, he is," says Destiny.

"He is always that good," says Julie. "This is the third game I've seen."

Katie comes back over and says, "You guys want to join us? We're going to head over to the burger joint across the street."

Destiny looks at Calix and he nods. "Sure," Destiny says to Katie.

"Great! Ready to go?"

"I want to check in with the sitter before we head over," says Destiny.

"Okay. Julie and I will head over and grab some tables for us. Meet us there?"

"Sure thing," says Destiny.

Destiny and Calix call Jennifer from Destiny's cell phone. She assures them everything is fine and that Georgia is sleeping soundly.

"Sleeping," says Calix as they hang up the phone. "Can you believe it. Maybe we should get Jennifer to move in."

"Yeah," says Destiny in a distant voice as she looks down the court at Fred. "No kidding."

"Everything okay?" asks Calix.

"I guess, but look at Fred." At least half a dozen girls are crowded around Fred and he is enjoying every minute of it. One girl in particular is really flirting with him. In fact, she is getting very friendly and Fred is soaking it up and getting friendly back.

"Oh, that's probably just fan stuff. Girls just love athletes. You know."

"Maybe, but it's not proper of him if he's dating Katie."

"I'm sure it's fine," says Calix.

Then one of the girls who was gathered around Fred walks past them and Destiny says, "Excuse me."

The girl stops and looks at Destiny. "Yeah?"

"Who is that girl over there with Fred? The one with her arm around him."

"Oh, that's Anabelle, his ex-girlfriend. She still real sweet on him."

"It' looks like he is still real sweet on her, too." Says Destiny.

"Oh yeah, for sure. He can't get enough of her," she says and before walking away.

Destiny huffs a big breath as she slings her purse over her shoulder. She can remember her boyfriend Curtis years ago and how he was dating other girls behind her back. "That is not going to happen to my friend," she says to Calix. "Katie needs to know about this."

"Do you think it's a good idea to get in the middle of it?"

"So, I should just let my friend get hurt? Just stand by and do nothing?"

"I guess not," replies Calix. "Just be careful."

"I will."

And with that, Destiny leads the way out of the gym and they head over to the burger joint.

✧ ✧ ✧

When they arrive at the burger place, there are a bunch of people congregated at a few tables at the back. The team is just starting to arrive, but Fred isn't there yet and Destiny knows why. Katie sees Destiny and Calix and waves them over.

"I saved a couple of seats for you guys," she says.

Five minutes later, Fred swaggers in with a big smile on his face. Katie gives him a hug and a kiss as he sits down.

"Fred," says Katie. "I want you to meet my friend, Destiny, and her husband, Calix."

"Hi, guys," says Fred, putting out his hand to shake theirs. "I have heard so much about you, especially Destiny, the wonder teacher."

"Nice to meet you," says Calix, shaking Fred's hand.

Destiny just sits there for a moment, completely silent, until Calix gives her a gentle nudge. "Oh, hi," says Destiny. She shakes Fred's hand and feels him give her hand a gentle squeeze. Destiny shudders.

Orders are placed and everyone is chatting. The place is noisy. Katie is between her and Fred and Julie is sitting on the other side of Fred. It is as plain as the nose on his face that Fred is flirting with Julie, but Katie seems oblivious to it.

When the waitress brings their food, Fred starts to flirt with her, too. He stands up, goes behind her, and reaches around her to grab some of the dishes and put them on the table.

"Well, thanks, sugar," the waitress says.

"Anytime," Fred responds.

Destiny is fuming. She looks at Calix and he shrugs. Katie still doesn't see it, or if she does, she is not letting on. Destiny can't imagine this is the first time something like this has happened. They've been dating for weeks.

After about 20 minutes, Destiny has only eaten half of her burger. She sits picking at her fries and Katie looks over at her. "Destiny, you're so quiet. Everything okay?"

"Oh, yeah," Destiny lies. "I'm just really tired. Georgia is teething these days and keeping us up at night."

"I bet she is getting so big. I haven't seen her in a few weeks."

"Oh, she is," says Destiny.

Then she turns to Calix and whispers to him. "I can't stand watching this any more. Let's go."

"You sure?"

Destiny nods. Then she turns back to Katie. "Hey," she practically has to shout because everyone is laughing at a joke Fred just told. "We are going to head home."

"Really? The night is just getting started."

"I know," says Destiny, "but like I said, I'm really tired. I need to catch up on my sleep."

"Okay," says Katie. Then she turns to Fred. "Fred! Destiny and Calix are heading home."

"So soon?" says Fred.

"Baby keeping us up at night," says Calix. "We need some shut eye."

"Parenthood," says Fred. "Better you than me, my friend." A lot of people around them laugh and he just takes it in stride and starts to tell another joke.

Once they are outside, Destiny says, "I just can't believe him, but even more, I can't believe Katie. What is she doing with him?"

"No idea," says Calix.

They walk to their car and get in. Destiny is silent, worrying about her friend all the way home.

Chapter 5
Realization

✧ ✧ ✧

It is the second month of the school year. Destiny is sitting at her desk one Monday morning, drinking tea and trying to focus on the work in front of her. She is tired. She was up half the night with Georgia and spent a large part of the weekend at the center. Their numbers have tripled in the last month. It has been insane. And what time she didn't spend at the center on the weekend, she spent working on her PhD. Later today she has a curriculum meeting with the math department and she needs to be ready for it because she is presenting some of her new ideas to the group.

She doesn't know how she can keep up the pace. She is beginning to realize she has bitten off more than she can chew when she hears a knock at her classroom door and Ethel pokes her head in.

"Morning, dear. In early to get ready for the meeting?"

"Yeah," answers Destiny with a yawn.

Ethel comes in and walks right up to Destiny's desk. She bends down and pears into Destiny's face. "You look like death. Do you get any sleep at all?"

"Not as much as I'd like these days," Destiny admits.

"You do too much, you know that?"

Destiny nods and yawns again. "I was actually just thinking about that. But I have what I have on my plate. I can't clean it off now."

"Honey, let me give you some friendly advice. You need to determine what your priorities are and you need to align your life with those."

"But everything I'm doing is important. I can't stop being a mother. I can't give up my job. My tutoring center isn't going anywhere and it's growing all the time. And I'm in the middle of my PhD, which will give me more and better career opportunities. I don't see how I can give any of it up."

"Well then, you need some help. You cannot do it all on your own."

"I am hiring more staff at the center," says Destiny.

"Well, that's a start. If you can spend less time there, you will have more time to work on your thesis. And get some help with Georgia. Goodness knows Calix can't handle it all."

"Yeah, I know," says Destiny. "We have a neighbor down the street who has offered to help out with Georgia."

"Then you're all set!"

"Well, we'll see," says Destiny. "I have to get through today first and that means getting through the meeting later today."

"You'll be fine, dear."

"As long as you get going so I can finish preparing for it," says Destiny with a wink.

"Message received loud and clear," says Ethel. "I'll leave you to it. But please remember what I said. Get the help you need."

Destiny smiles. "Thanks, Ethel. I will. I promise."

Ethel trots on out of the classroom and Destiny smiles, grateful to have such good work colleagues.

✦ ✦ ✦

When dinner is finished that evening and they are cleaning up, Destiny asks Calix what he thinks of getting Madeline to help out with Georgia. Madeline Roberts is a retired teacher that lives three houses down and she loves Georgia with a passion. She is always dropping by. She says it's just to say hi, but Destiny knows it's really so she can see Georgia as much as she possibly can. She has offered to watch her multiple times in the past.

"I think it's a good idea," says Calix. "My hours will be picking up soon and I'll be working a lot of weekends. We could use the help."

"Okay, I'll pop down and see her after we're finished here."

"You go ahead," says Calix, taking the dishes out of Destiny's hands. "I can finish up here."

Destiny gives Calix a kiss on the cheek. Then she checks on Georgia, who is playing happily on a blanket on the dining room floor. When she steps outside, she stands on the doorstep for a moment. It is a lovely evening. The air is warm and a few puffy clouds are floating lazily across the sky. A soft breeze ruffles the leaves of the trees.

But Destiny isn't outside to enjoy the beauty of the evening. She walks down the steps and up the sidewalk to Madeline's house. The little red brick house looks inviting. Lace curtains hang in the window above a flower garden that is full of flowers of all kinds, strategically organized to be pleasing to the eye.

Destiny knocks on the door of the house. A moment later, Madeline opens the door and smiles. "Honey, it's about time."

"Hi, Madeline. What do you mean, it's about time?"

"I've been waiting for you to come over and ask for some help with that sweet little thing."

Destiny laughs. "Have you, now?"

"Oh, yes. I watch you juggle everything. I see how you are running yourself ragged. It was only a matter of time before you came knocking on my door. Now, come on in so we can make some arrangements."

Inside, Destiny sits at the dining table and Madeline makes tea. Then she places tea in front of each of them and sits across from Destiny. As she pours a little milk in her tea, she says, "When do you need me?"

Just like that. No worry about scheduling. No availability times. "We don't want to impose, Madeline."

"Hogwash. All I do is sit around here anyway. I might as well do that with some good company and Georgia is good company."

"Well, probably some evenings and some time on the weekends. Calix is going to be working more hours soon and I have to focus on my PhD and the center."

"Honey, don't you worry. You just settle the times that you need me and I will make sure I'm available. I have far more flexibility than you."

"You are amazing," says Destiny, breathing an inward sigh of relief. How she got so fortunate to have such a wonderful neighbor in her life she will never know.

"I'm just doing my neighborly duty. We need to watch out for each other. That's how it's always been."

"Well, Calix and I really appreciate it," says Destiny as she sips her tea. "And we are happy to pay you."

At that, Madeline's eyebrows shoot up and she peers at Destiny over the rim of her glasses. Destiny knows Madeline won't accept a penny and she doesn't say another word about it. She'll find other ways to repay Madeline.

✧ ✧ ✧

That evening, after Georgia is in bed and Calix is watching television, Destiny sits down to do some of her PhD work. She opens her books and turns on the computer, then she just sits there and stares at the computer screen.

She feels better about things now that she knows they can rely on Madeline, but she still feels overwhelmed. She is dangerously close to falling behind with her coursework. But even more important is the fact that the center is growing so fast. Destiny feels she can hardly keep up. Plus, having more students means she should be there more often, not less.

Destiny knows more staff is needed at the center. Maybe she should hire a manager, or better yet, promote one of her current staff to management. That would make things easier.

As Destiny sits and thinks about the idea, a vision forms in her mind. In it, she sees Alvin. She has called him to ask for his help and he has come through for her. Alvin always comes through for her and she knows it.

She sees him in the center, talking to a family and working with the staff and students. He looks happy and smiles at everyone. And she knows that is exactly how he would be. He would have a lot of fun helping out at the center.

The vision leaves her and Destiny shakes her head. She will obviously have to get by without Alvin. Besides, she hasn't spoken with him in a while. She isn't even sure what he's doing right now. Last she heard, he was in Austin working as an engineering consultant.

Destiny has a family and a life here and she needs to focus on that. And at this very moment, she needs to focus on the work in front of her. Destiny tries to get something done. She lasts for about a half an hour, then she gives up. She is just too tired.

Destiny decides to go to bed early. She kisses Calix goodnight and gets ready. She practically falls asleep as soon as her head hits the pillow. And she dreams of a clock that has 36 hours on it.

Chapter 6
Party Pooper

✧ ✧ ✧

A couple of weeks have passed and Destiny finds things going a little easier now that Madeline is taking care of Georgia on a regular basis. Destiny has promoted Shelley to assistant manager at the tutoring center and increased Reginae's hours so she works more hours on Saturdays, as well as Thursday and Friday evenings.

Unfortunately, at school things haven't changed. Principal Brandfather is still intruding on Destiny's space, watching her and making unannounced visits to her classroom. Destiny has even seen her talking to her students and she is sure Principal Brandfather is trying to find out if any of them have had any problems in her class.

But it's a beautiful day and Destiny is heading outside to eat her lunch before she does lunch duty on the schoolyard. As she walks outside the school, the sunshine hits her face and feels wonderful. At the same moment, her cell phone rings.

Destiny pulls her phone out of her pocket and answers it as she crosses the street to the park. "Hello," she says as she finds an available bench.

"Destiny!" It's Katie and Destiny groans inwardly at having to speak to her. She has hardly spoken to Katie since the night of the basketball game, when she met Fred. She has made all sorts of excuses about how busy she is, which were at least partly true. At least that's how Destiny justifies her avoidance of Katie to herself.

"Hi, Katie. How are you?"

"I'm great. Did I catch you at a bad time?"

As much as she wants to lie, Destiny says, "No, I'm just about to have lunch. I can talk for a minute."

"I won't keep you long," says Katie. "I'm having a party this weekend and I want you and Calix to come."

"A party. That sounds fun, but I don't know..."

"Oh, please, Destiny! I really want you guys to come. I know you're busy, but you said you need to relax more often. There will be loads of people there and a friend of Fred's is in a band and they're going to play for us."

At the mention of Fred, Destiny's blood runs cold. But she knows this is important to Katie. "Okay, I'll see what I can do. I'm sure we can swing by, at least for a little while."

"Awesome! It's on Saturday night anytime after 8:00. See you then!"

"Sounds good," says Destiny. They say goodbye and Destiny puts her phone away. As she takes a bite of her sandwich, Destiny wonders how she will make it through an evening watching Fred make a fool of Katie while Katie seems oblivious.

Then Destiny sees Ethel crossing the street. When she reaches Destiny, she says, "May I join you?"

"Of course," Destiny replies. "Pull up a bench."

"Chatting with Calix, were you? I saw you tucking away your phone," Ethel says as if she needs to explain herself.

"No, to my friend, Katie."

"You don't sound very thrilled about it."

"Well, it's a bit of a story really. She is dating a guy who is, well, as sleazy as they come. Flirts with other girls right in front of her and she doesn't even seem to notice."

"Oh, I've seen that type before. Both the man and the woman, mind you. He just loves the attention and the power, and as for her, well, maybe she doesn't want to see."

"What do you mean?" asks Destiny.

"Well, she just might be so happy to have a man in her life that she is willing to overlook the obvious. Maybe she feels validated just being his girlfriend."

"Katie wouldn't do that. I mean, I know she's had trouble with boyfriends in the past and she would really like to settle down and get married, but I can't believe she would settle for the likes of Fred."

"Well, I don't know her so I can't say, but I hope you're right."

Their conversation turns to school-related matters and 15 minutes later, Destiny's lunch has been put away and she is on schoolyard. As she watches kids climb all over the monkey bars, she thinks about what Ethel said. Could Katie really be ignoring what is happening?

No way, thinks Destiny. *Katie is smarter than that. But then why is she still with Fred?*

✧ ✧ ✧

The doorbell rings at 7:45. It's Madeline. She agreed to watch Georgia at their place tonight so Georgia could go to sleep in her crib.

"Thanks so much for doing this," says Calix.

"You know I'm always here for the little one," says Madeline, reaching out and taking Georgia from Destiny. "Who better to hang out with on a Saturday night?"

"Well, we really appreciate it," says Destiny as she slips on her shoes. "I don't imagine we'll be out that late."

"Now don't you hurry home on account of me," says Madeline. "I'm just fine until whenever."

"Actually, it's not you I'm worried about."

"That boyfriend of Katie's? What's his name? Fred?"

Destiny nods.

"Never mind him, just go and have a good time."

"I'll try," says Destiny. She kisses Georgia and she and Calix get into the car.

"How long do you wager we'll be at the party?" Destiny asks Calix.

"Not very long."

They pull out of their driveway and head in the direction of Katie's house. It's going to feel like a long night, even if they cut it short.

✧ ✧ ✧

Calix parks on the street a couple of houses down from Katie's house. They can hear music coming from Katie's backyard, and as they approach the house, they can hear a bunch of people laughing like they just heard a great joke.

"Probably the same lame joke he told after the game that night," says Destiny. Calix snickers.

When they reach the front door, they find a note that reads:

Just come around to the back, folks!

Calix shrugs and they make their way around to the gate that leads into the backyard. When they open the gate. Destiny is surprised to see so many people. There has to be at least 50. She was expecting something a little less over-the-top.

"Destiny!" Katie spots them and runs over to greet them. "You made it!"

Entangled in a hug from Katie, Destiny says, "Yes, we managed."

"Great. Hey Calix. The party's hopping! Come and get something to drink."

Calix follows the two friends as they make their way to the far side of the patio. "Who *are* all these people?" asks Destiny.

"Oh, people from the basketball team and a bunch of Fred's friends."

Destiny looks around, amazed. Her eyes land on Fred's ex-girlfriend, the one she saw him with after the basketball game. She hardly recognizes anyone. Julie is dancing with some guy Destiny has never laid eyes on and there are a few people from her old school. That's it.

"Hey, Fred," yells Katie as she points to Destiny. Fred saunters over.

"Hey there," he says. "Good to see you again, uh…"

"Destiny," says Destiny with a slight edge to her voice.

"Right, Destiny and hubby. The folks with the baby."

"That's us," says Calix, then he turns so only Destiny can see his face and rolls his eyes. Destiny holds back a giggle. "What do you want to drink?" Calix asks her.

"Oh, I don't know. Ice tea or soda. Surprise me."

Fred has already disappeared because the band is tuning up, and within a couple of minutes, they begin to play. People are flocking to the lawn so they can dance. The music isn't bad and Destiny is nodding her head in time with the beat when Calix brings back their drinks.

"Come and dance?" asks Katie.

"In a little while," says Destiny.

"Okay, I'm gone." Katie dances and sways her way into the crowd of people.

"She looks so happy," says Destiny. "I just don't get it."

"Maybe she is," Calix replies.

"Ethel thinks maybe she is deliberately avoiding the knowledge of what Fred is like because she is just happy to have scored a man."

"What do you think?"

"I don't know."

After about five minutes, Calix takes Destiny's drink and sets it on a table with his. He holds out his hand. "We can at least try to have some fun. You know, since we are out like two parents without their kid."

Destiny laughs and takes his hand. He leads her into the dancing crowd and Destiny begins to dance. At first, she feels uncomfortable, but soon she is totally letting loose. She hasn't danced like this in a few years.

After a while, Calix excuses himself because he has to visit the washroom. Destiny starts to head out of the dance area when Fred appears in front of her.

"Hey there, pretty lady," he says.

"Uh, hey," says Destiny, trying to navigate around Fred's huge frame.

"Where are you going? I was gonna come dance with you." He sounds almost shocked that a woman would walk away from the dance floor when she has a chance to dance with him.

"Oh, I need a break."

Fred grabs her hand and tugs her toward the dance area, but Destiny yanks her hand back. "I said no!"

"Okay, okay. But I'd really love to groove with you. You're a real cutie."

"I'm a married cutie," says Destiny through gritted teeth.

"Sure, whatever," says Fred and then he is gone.

By the time Calix gets back, Destiny is fuming. "Let's go," she says.

"Yeah?"

"Yeah." She starts walking toward the gate.

"You gonna say goodbye to Katie?"

"No."

In the car, Calix sits for a moment. "Is everything alright?" he asks.

"Fred made a pass at me."

"What?"

Destiny nods.

"I'll take care of him," says Calix, reaching for the door handle.

"No, just take me home."

Calix pauses. "Yeah, sure." He starts the car.

"Tomorrow, I'm going to have to think how to break it to Katie that her boyfriend is a jerk."

And I don't know how to do that, thinks Destiny.

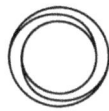

Part 3:
Conference

Chapter 7

Big News

✧ ✧ ✧

Destiny spends the following week fretting over how to talk to Katie about Fred. *He hit on me*, Destiny thinks for the thousandth time, *one of Katie's best friends! What was he thinking?*

This thought keeps bouncing around in her head as she walks up the stairs to her classroom on Monday morning. As she reaches the top of the stairs, Destiny's cell phone rings. She answers it as she walks into her classroom. "Hello?"

"Hello. Is this Destiny Sycamores?"

"Yes, it is. Who may I ask is calling?"

"My name is Caroline Brimstone and I am calling to invite you to the Professional Annual Tutoring Conference that is taking place in New Orleans."

"Really? That sounds wonderful!" says Destiny. "When is the conference?"

"Late next month. October 26 to 29. And we would dearly love for you to give a presentation on the work you've been doing. We'll email you all the details."

"Four days," says Destiny, wondering how she can pull it off. "Yes, I'd love to. Thank you." She hasn't actually figured out how she will manage to make it to the conference, but she knows she has to be there.

"That's wonderful," says Caroline. "We'll be in touch."

"Yes, thank you." Destiny hangs up and smiles. What a great way to escape the craziness of life. Although, four days away will actually add to the craziness in the end.

Four days! Destiny is going to need time off for the conference. *Oh no*, Destiny thinks. *Principal Brandfather will never let me have four days off.*

Now, Destiny has something new to worry about. Getting time off for the conference. But to be able to hear what other people are doing in the tutoring and education industry and to be able to present the work she has been doing would be a dream come true.

Destiny knows she absolutely must find a way to make this work. She will discuss it with Calix tonight and then speak with Principal Brandfather tomorrow.

✧ ✧ ✧

The next morning, Destiny goes into the office. Sheree is away from her desk so Destiny peeks into Principal Brandfather's office and finds her at her desk.

Principal Brandfather looks up. "Hello, Destiny. What can I do for you?" She barely makes eye contact, as usual.

"Hi Daniella." The butterflies in Destiny's stomach threaten to fly right out of her. "I have come to ask you for some time off."

"Time off? I see. So, it turns out you can't handle the insane schedule you have. What is this to be? Sick leave?"

"Oh, no. Nothing like that," says Destiny. "I received a phone call yesterday inviting me to a tutoring conference that is taking place in New Orleans next month. They want me to give a presentation. I know it might be an imposition and I'm sorry. I'll have to take a few days away from my PhD work, too. But this conference is really an incredible opportunity."

"You are working on your PhD?" says Principal Brandfather. She makes no attempt to hide the surprise in her voice, but she also doesn't sound disapproving the way she usually does."

"Yes. I am studying at Nova Southeastern University in Fort Lauderdale, Florida."

"Really." She sounds thoughtful. "I'm also working on my PhD."

"I didn't know that," says Destiny, thinking they finally have something in common. "I'd love to talk about what you are working on sometime."

"That would be good," says Principal Brandfather. "It's always good to get a colleague's opinion of your work."

Did she just refer to me as a colleague? thinks Destiny.

"So, about the time off for the conference?"

"When exactly?" asks Principal Brandfather.

"October 26 to 29. I'd need that plus travel time."

Principal Brandfather looks at her schedule. "There doesn't seem to be anything major going on here at the school so I don't see a problem with it. However, I would like you to share what you learn at the conference with everyone at a staff meeting. If you are going to take time off for this, then at least we can all benefit."

"Yes! Of course!" says Destiny. "I'd be happy to." Principal Brandfather said yes! Destiny could just kiss the woman, although that might make her change her mind in a hurry.

Destiny practically dances out of Principal Brandfather's office. Sheree is at her desk and looks at Destiny with an odd look on her face. "It's not often I see you come out of her office with a smile on your face," Sheree whispers. "What happened in there?"

"She actually gave me time off to go to a conference next month."

Sheree's eyebrows shoot up and her mouth forms an O. then she gives Destiny a thumbs-up. Destiny waves and carries on up to her classroom to get on with her morning prep.

✧ ✧ ✧

Destiny spends the next few weeks getting ready for the conference. She wants to give an incredible presentation and that means putting a lot of effort into what she is doing. It also means she is missing more time from her PhD work, something she hadn't considered.

However, it's worth it. By the time a week before the conference arrives, Destiny is ready. And she has also noticed that Principal Brandfather has been a lot easier on her since their conversation. In fact, the change came after she learned Destiny is doing her PhD. Did that fact make Destiny better or more professional in Principal Brandfather's mind? It almost seems as if Principal Brandfather takes Destiny more seriously, now.

Principal Brandfather even goes out of her way to make polite conversation with Destiny. Destiny is fine with that, whatever the reason. Having Principal Brandfather off her back and on her side is a true miracle.

Chapter 8

Conference

✧ ✧ ✧

Before Destiny knows it, the weeks have passed and it is time to leave for the conference. Destiny and Calix had decided to leave Friday right after school. They will take Georgia and drive to Many, Louisiana to visit her family before heading to New Orleans.

As they pull out of their driveway to begin their journey, Destiny looks back at Georgia, who is staring out the window as she plays with her feet. Destiny wonders what Georgia can possibly be looking at because all she can really see out the window is blue sky and maybe the tops of a few trees.

"Nice day for a drive," says Destiny.

Calix nods and says, "You gonna be okay leaving her?"

Destiny looks back at Georgia again. "I'll manage." They decided they would leave Georgia with Momma and Pop while they are at the conference. Destiny has never been away from Georgia overnight, let alone four days. She can already feel the ache of anxiety in her chest, but pushes it away, knowing Georgia will be fine with Momma.

After hours of driving and a number of stops to feed and change Georgia, they arrive at Destiny's parents' home. Momma, Pop, and Destiny's sister Michelle are waiting on the front steps. By the time Destiny opens her door to get out of the truck, Momma is taking Georgia right out of her car seat.

"Momma!" says Destiny. "Thank goodness she was awake."

"Don't you worry, child," says Momma. "I know what I'm doin'. Now give your Momma a kiss!"

Destiny kisses and hugs Momma and then Pop has his arms around her. Momma greets Calix and then she says, "Now, I'm gonna go stare at my grandbaby for a while."

Michelle has been waiting for a hug and Destiny embraces her. "It's so good to see you," says Michelle.

"You, too!"

"Hey there, Calix," says Michelle, giving him a hug. "You taking good care of my little sis?"

"Sure am," he says. Then he and Pop shake hands. Michelle is already over beside Momma, talking to Georgia.

Calix takes Destiny's hand. "I'm not sure whether you'll even see her while we're here," he says, nodding toward Momma and Michelle doting on Georgia.

"I think you might be right," says Destiny. They get their bags and everyone heads inside.

As soon as they walk through the door, Destiny can smell something delicious. "Oh, Momma! Is that jambalaya?"

"It sure is."

"Oh, I've missed your cooking!"

"Well, enjoy it, sugar. But you gonna have to serve yourself because I ain't lettin' go of this baby."

Destiny laughs. They all serve themselves and sit down at the table. It's the best dinner Destiny has had in a long time. There is just something about coming home to Momma's cooking.

✧ ✧ ✧

On Sunday morning, Destiny and Calix get ready to leave. Georgia has taken to Momma so much, Destiny knows she'll be fine. "I don't even think she'll know we're gone," Destiny says to Calix as they put their suitcase in the truck.

Calix laughs. "And I don't know if your Momma is going to give her back."

"No kidding!"

Saying goodbye to Georgia is the hardest thing Destiny has ever done. Georgia is sleeping as Destiny gently kisses her forehead. Calix does the same. Then he takes her hand and pulls her from the house. Once they are on the road, Destiny has tears streaming down her cheeks.

"She'll be fine," says Calix.

"Oh, I know. I mean, she's with Momma and Pop. I trust them totally. I'm just going to miss her so much."

"I know, but we get some time together. It's been too long."

Destiny smiles and takes Calix's hand. "Yes, it has. Let's make the most of it."

The drive to New Orleans takes five hours, which includes a short stop for lunch at a roadside diner. When they arrive, Destiny realizes it's been a long time since she was in New Orleans.

Calix drives into downtown and turns into the French Quarter. "Where are we going?" asks Destiny.

"To our hotel," Calix replies. Calix was the one who booked their room and Destiny didn't really know what part of town they were staying in. The French Quarter is very nice and Destiny begins to get very excited.

Their hotel is lovely and Destiny looks around at the ornate lobby as they check in. Their room is stunning and overlooks the Mississippi River. "This is perfect," says Destiny and for a while she forgets about how much she misses Georgia.

Calix hugs her and says, "I thought you deserved a nice trip and a little bit of luxury."

"Thank you."

"And now we will change into something nice and go have dinner."

"Change? It's that fancy?"

"It sure is. I made reservations two weeks ago."

They change into nice clothes. Calix wears a pair of casual dressy pants, a t-shirt, and a sports jacket. Destiny wears a flowered skirt, a blouse, and a blue sweater. Looking dashing, they walk down the street to the restaurant.

When they enter the restaurant, a man greets them and Calix gives them his name. "Ah, yes," says the man. "Just follow me, please."

They are given a window table and a candle is lit. "This is beautiful," says Destiny. "Thank you so much!"

"My pleasure," says Calix.

A waiter comes along. "Good evening. I am Andrew and I will be your waiter this evening."

They order drinks and then decide to share a few dishes, including an incredible seafood appetizer. Destiny's mouth is watering as she waits for the food. When it arrives, Destiny says,

"This is almost too gorgeous to eat!" But she digs in and has no trouble ruining the picturesque presentation of the food.

When dinner is done, Destiny and Calix walk arm-in-arm through the French Quarter, enjoying the architecture and the beautiful evening. But it isn't long before they go back to the room and settle in for the night. Destiny has a big day tomorrow.

✧ ✧ ✧

Destiny arrives at the conference at 8:00 am the following morning. She is rested and ready to go and she is so excited about the presentations she is going to see.

Each presentation she attends throughout the day gives her new insight into the tutoring world. She learns a lot that she hadn't realized, including some of the problems frequently encountered by tutoring programs.

When Calix catches up with her at the end of the first day, she is deep in thought. "Hey," he says. "You look like you are processing something pretty big in that brain of yours."

Destiny gives Calix a hug. "Yeah, I guess I am."

As they walk to a nearby restaurant to have some dinner, Destiny says, "I've been thinking about writing a tutoring book, something that can instruct the education community on proper practices, curriculum, and how tutoring fits in with standard education."

"You've mentioned it before, but you haven't spoken about it much."

"Well, you know how busy I've been. But from what I've seen today, the book I envision is really needed."

"Then do it. Write it."

Open Your
Eyes
and Visualize

"I will. But first I have to get through my presentation tomorrow."

"You'll do just fine."

When Tuesday morning arrives, Destiny is standing at the front of the auditorium, a bundle of nerves dressed in a nice pantsuit. As the room fills up, Destiny's nervousness grows. Then the lights dim slightly and she is set to begin.

"Hello everyone and welcome to my presentation entitled *Open Your Eyes and Visualize*." As she speaks, her nervousness dissipates and her passion begins to pour through her words. It is clear how much she believes in what she is saying and the audience is hanging on her every word.

When she wraps up, Destiny is greeted with thunderous applause. She feels truly wonderful, and as she goes on through the day, many people come up to talk to her about her presentation and to get her thoughts on different aspects of tutoring and curriculum development.

On Wednesday, Destiny enjoys more presentations and solidifies her desire to write her book. She and Calix enjoy the gala dinner on Wednesday evening. It is an important part of the conference. The conference is to end at noon on Thursday, but they leave first thing Thursday morning. Destiny is anxious to see Georgia so they drive straight through with only one stop to get some gas and some snacks for the road.

As soon as they pull into her parents' driveway, Destiny flies out of the truck and into the house. "Hello child," says Momma.

"Hi Momma," says Destiny, scooping up Georgia and hugging her tight.

"She was just fine, just fine," says Pop.

"I know she was, Pop, but I missed her so much."

Momma and Pop are smiling.

"She grew," says Destiny as Calix comes in. "I swear she grew in the few days we've been gone. What have you been feeding her Momma?"

They all laugh. And after a last night with Destiny's family, she and Calix and little Georgia set out for home bright and early on Saturday morning.

Chapter 9
Fred

✧ ✧ ✧

A few months have passed since the conference and the end of the school year is in sight. Destiny has tried her best to avoid spending time with Katie and especially Fred. He makes her skin crawl every time she sees him.

"You're going to have to tell her," Calix had told her. "It's eating you up."

He was right, of course. So, when Katie asked Destiny to meet for lunch on Saturday, Destiny said yes. But now Destiny is driving to the café where they agreed to meet and she is waffling on her decision to tell Katie what's been going on. After all, what if Katie doesn't believe her? What if she gets upset? Then again, what if she is grateful?

Destiny isn't sure what to do. As she pulls into the café parking lot, she decides she needs to tell Katie, regardless of the consequences. Yet, when she walks into the café and sees Katie sitting and waiting for her at the table, her resolve crumbles.

✧ ✧ ✧

Once they say hi and hug, they sit down and look at the menu. Destiny doesn't feel very hungry so she just orders a salad and an ice tea. Katie orders a burger and fries.

Destiny decides to fish around and find out if Katie's relationship with Fred is still blissful. If it isn't, then maybe telling her will be easy. "So, how are things with Fred?" she asks.

"Oh Destiny," says Katie. "It's better than ever. Honestly, Destiny, I think he is the one. We are so into each other."

Destiny almost gags on her salad. How can Katie be so blind? "Have you met Annabelle?" asks Destiny. "I remember meeting her at the game, the night I met Fred."

"Oh her," replies Katie with acid dripping from every word. "Yeah, I've met her. Fred can't seem to get rid of her. I mean really, can't she see he has someone new?"

"He doesn't want anything to do with her?"

"Of course not! He's totally cool and has reassured me so many times that I am his one and only."

"Katie," says Destiny.

Katie looks at her, waiting to hear what she has to say, but Destiny just can't do it. "I just need to go to the washroom. I'll be right back."

"Sure, okay. I'll be here," she says with a smile.

Destiny goes to the washroom and stands at the sink looking in the mirror. *What am I going to do?* she wonders. *How do I tell her and break her heart? Katie will be devastated.*

But then Destiny realizes that it's not her that will be breaking Katie's heart. That is all on Fred. And Katie has the right to know what he's been up to. Destiny decides that she absolutely has to tell Katie everything. So, she takes a deep breath and heads back out to the table.

✧ ✧ ✧

Destiny sits down, takes another deep breath, and starts talking before she can change her mind and before Katie can say anything. "Katie, Fred is not the right guy for you. He's not good enough."

"What are you talking about, Destiny?"

"Listen, the night I met Fred, when were at the game and you went on ahead to the restaurant, I saw him flirting with Annabelle. He was totally into her and he definitely didn't have a problem with her flirting with him. Some woman who passed by told me he is still into Annabelle."

"Destiny, you're wrong."

"No, I'm not. At the restaurant that night he was flirting with the waitress and I have seen him flirt with plenty of people, right in front of you! I don't know how you don't see it. And at your party last fall, he made a pass at me, even though he knows I'm married and have a baby."

Katie sits in silence for a moment, as if she is contemplating what Destiny has said. Destiny is just waiting for her to say she had her suspicions, anything but what she says next.

"You know, Destiny. I have always been supportive of you. When things went bad between you and Julie, I was always on your side. When you had a hard time with work and with Principal Brandfather, I was always there. I have bent over backward to hold you up to everyone who doubted you or were jealous. And now you are stabbing me in the back."

Destiny is stunned. "Katie, no. I…"

"What is it? Are you jealous of Fred? Is that it? That he has something more going for him than a construction job? That he is a better catch?"

"Hold on right there," says Destiny. "I have nothing to be jealous of. I have a wonderful life with a terrific husband, a beautiful daughter, and a fabulous career. I am only saying this because I care about you and you need to know."

"You care? It's like you can't stand to see someone as happy as you are." Just a moment ago she was calling Destiny jealous, now she is saying Destiny is happy in her life. Katie clearly is grasping. Maybe she really does know what is going on and is turning a blind eye.

"I want you to be happy, Katie. But how can you be happy with a guy that is still into his ex-girlfriend, who flirts with every woman he sees right in front of you, and who hits on your best friend?"

"Best friend? Oh, he didn't hit on my best friend, because we aren't friends anymore."

"What? Katie, come on!"

Katie puts up her hand to signal the waitress. "Can I have my bill, please."

"Katie, don't do this. Let's talk about it."

"There is nothing to talk about."

Destiny just sits there and watches as Katie gets the money out for her bill and leaves it on the table. Then she stands up, ready to leave.

"So, that's it then?" says Destiny. "Years of friendship gone because you are too blind to see how badly a guy you've known for a few months is treating you and you won't trust the best friend who is trying to help?"

"Like I said, we aren't friends anymore. Unless you are willing to support my relationship with Fred and put all of this nonsense out of play."

"I can't do that, Katie. I can't sit by and watch him do this to you. I mean, just ask some of your other friends. I can't be the only one who has seen it."

"All of my other friends adore Fred. It's just you, Destiny. And I'm done with you."

Katie turns and walks away, leaving Destiny sitting at the table shaking with anger and frustration. She doesn't understand how that went so wrong. She only wanted to help.

The waitress brings her bill. "Trouble?" she asks.

"Yeah," says Destiny. "Her boyfriend treats her so badly and she won't see it. I tried to tell her, but..."

"People aren't going to see things they don't want to see," says the waitress. Destiny remembers her conversation with Ethel a few months ago and what Ethel had said.

"Well, she just might be so happy to have a man in her life that she is willing to overlook the obvious. Maybe she feels validated just being his girlfriend."

Maybe it's true. Destiny pays her bill and leaves the restaurant. She feels a big hole in her life and she hopes Katie isn't gone for good.

Chapter 10

Epilogue

✧ ✧ ✧

Destiny walks out of the school on her last day of work. Summer vacation has arrived and everything at the school has bee wrapped up. She waves at Ethel as she walks to her truck. The year ended on a perfect note. At the year-end assembly, she found out her students had the top marks in the district. Principal Brandfather praised her efforts and her results in front of the whole school.

Now, as she gets into her truck, she can focus on her other responsibilities. She is looking forward to spending more time at the center. She misses the kids there and hasn't seen much of them over the past few months. Of course, Shelley has been doing fantastic job managing everything. The center has run smoothly and the numbers have continued to grow.

When she pulls into the driveway, Calix is sitting on the front step and Georgia is standing in front of him, each of her little hands holding onto one of his index fingers. She has a big smile on her face as she sees Destiny get out of the truck and she starts bouncing up and down.

Destiny walks over until she is just a few steps away from Georgia and drops her bag and purse. Then she squats down and holds out her arms, "Come see Mama," she says to Georgia.

Georgia's smile widens and she takes a halting step toward Destiny. Georgia took her first step at the beginning of the week and has been working on it every since. Now, she slowly covers the distance between Destiny and Calix, and when she reaches Destiny, Destiny gathers her into her arms and covers her in kisses.

"Good for you, Georgia!" says Destiny. "You keep working hard and you can do anything."

Then she looks up and smiles at Calix. "It's finally summer vacation," he says. "Now maybe you can slow down a bit."

They look at each other for a moment and then they burst out laughing. Destiny will never slow down. She knows it and Calix knows it. It just isn't in her nature. But she will be able to spend more time at home.

They will have a few weeks in Fort Lauderdale again this summer, but around that Destiny will focus on making some changes at the center, working on her thesis, and writing her book. But most of all, she wants to soak up her family, especially since Georgia is growing so fast. The last thing she wants is to look back in a few years and feel like she missed Georgia's childhood.

Destiny picks up Georgia and Calix grabs her bag and purse. Then they go into the house together. Destiny had already decided she wasn't doing anything that evening except spending time with her family.

"Maybe we should take a nice evening walk to thve park after dinner," says Calix.

"I think that's the prefect way to kick off the summer," says Destiny as she gives Georgia a kiss on the cheek.

www.ingramcontent.com/pod-product-compliance
Lightning Source LLC
Chambersburg PA
CBHW060709030426
42337CB00017B/2807